FAMOUS PEOPLE
FAMOUS LIVES

Biographies of famous people to support
the National Curriculum.

Louis
Braille

by Tessa Potter

Illustrations by Helena Owen

First published in 1996
by Franklin Watts
This edition 2002

Franklin Watts
96 Leonard Street
London EC2A 4XD

Franklin Watts Australia
56 O'Riordan Street
Alexandria, Sydney
NSW 2015

ISBN 0 7496 4352 8 (pbk)

A CIP catalogue record for this book is
available from the British Library

Dewey Decimal Classification
Number: 362.4

Series Editor: Sarah Ridley
Series Designer: Kirstie Billingham
Consultants: David Wray & Dr Anne Millard

Printed in Great Britain

Louis Braille

This is the story of Louis Braille, a blind French boy who became famous all over the world.

He invented a way to help blind people read and write.

Louis was born in a small
French village in 1809.

He was the Braille family's
fourth child. His brother and
sisters were much older than him.

Louis' family lived in a farm house. They had some land and kept hens and a cow.

Louis' father made saddles and harnesses for horses.

Little Louis was a bright, happy
child. He liked helping his
mother and father. He wanted
to have a go at everything.

8

9

One day, when he was three, something terrible happened.

Louis was alone in his father's workshop. He wanted to cut some leather like his father. He climbed up onto a stool.

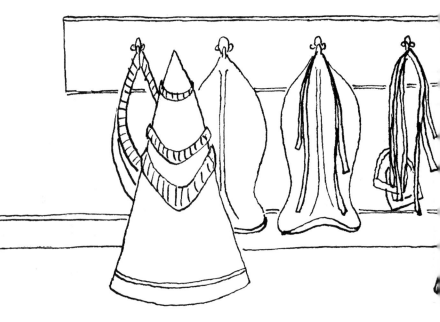

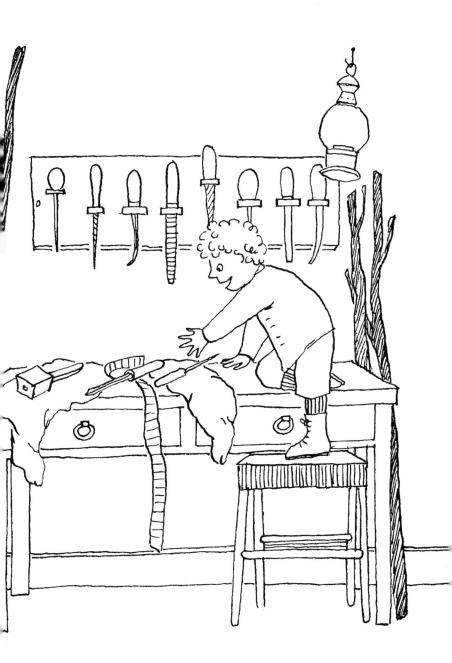

11

He took a sharp tool from the bench. The leather was very tough. The tool slipped ...

This is hard work...

Louis' father and mother heard
a scream. They ran into the
workshop. Blood was running
down Louis' face. His eye was
badly cut.

14

Louis' eye became infected. There was nothing the doctors could do. The infection spread to his good eye.

Louis began to see less and less.
By the time he was five years
old, he was blind.

Louis' mother and father were
very sad. What would become
of their Louis?

Would he become a poor beggar,
like the blind man they saw at
the market?

19

Louis had to learn to live in
a new dark world.

He had to learn how to do
everything again. He learnt
now by touching and listening.

20

Louis learnt quickly and was soon able to help his family again.

The village priest saw how
clever Louis was and wanted to
help him. He taught him stories
from the Bible.

He taught him the sounds of different birds and animals.

It's a blackbird.

When Louis was seven, a new school teacher came to the village. He welcomed Louis to the village school.

Louis couldn't read or write like other children but he remembered everything he heard. Soon he was top of the class.

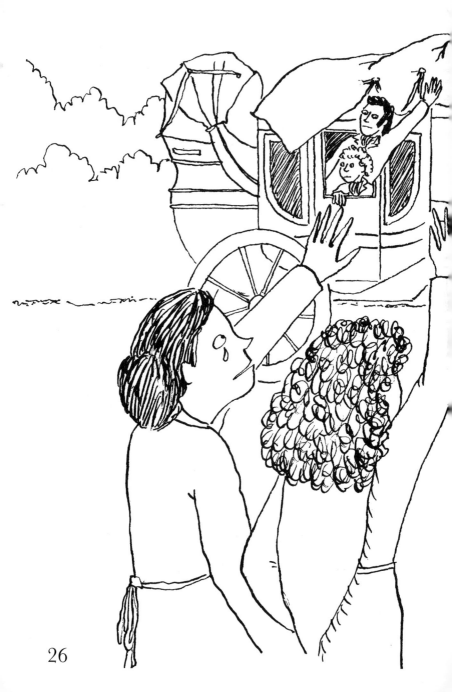

When he was ten, a place was
found for Louis at a special
school for blind children in Paris.

He was sad to leave his home
and family but excited about the
new school.

The school in the city was strange and the teachers very strict. The building was huge, cold and damp.

Louis couldn't find his way
round at first but he soon made
a friend, called Gabriel.

Louis loved the geography,
history and mathematics lessons.

He learnt how to make baskets
and slippers.

He learnt to play the piano.

He was a very bright pupil.
There were even a few special
books at the school so he could
learn to read. The books were
very big with raised letters.
It took a long time to feel and
read a word.

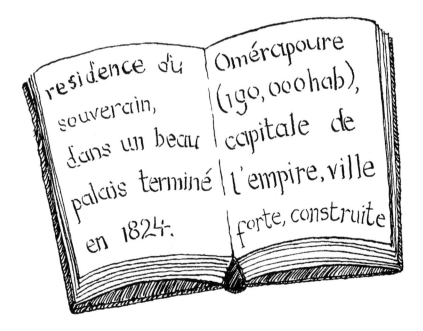

résidence du souverain, dans un beau palais terminé en 1824.

Omérapoure (190,000hab), capitale de l'empire, ville forte, construite

When Louis was twelve, an army officer called Charles Barbier came to the school. He had invented a way for soldiers to pass secret instructions to each other at night.

He thought this 'Night-writing'
might help blind people to read
and write. Dots and dashes for
different sounds were punched
into paper tape.

Louis was very excited by this new way of reading. He and his friends could even write to each other now.

But Barbier's system was very
complicated. It used a lot of dots.

Louis wanted to find a quicker
easier way.

Louis spent the next months trying to invent his own system. He worked late into the night and through his summer holidays. He knew the system had to be easy and quick to learn and use.

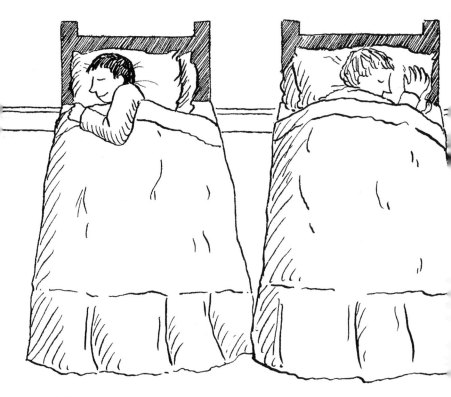

After two years, Louis had perfected a simple way to write every letter of the alphabet. His system used only six raised dots, like the dots on a domino.
By running your finger gently across the dots you could 'read' the letters.

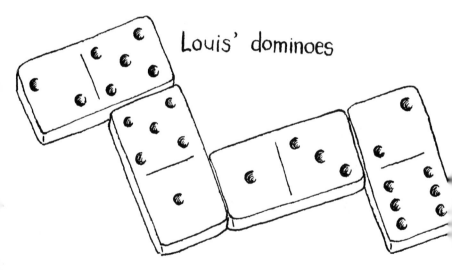

Louis' dominoes

His friends quickly learnt the new method.

Louis later became a teacher at the school but it was still a long time before his system was used by everyone. People who were not blind did not understand how important Louis' work was.

Louis spent the rest of his life
teaching at the school. For many
years only his friends and pupils
used Louis' method of reading
and writing. They tried hard to
make other people use it too.

Louis was often very ill. He died when he was only forty-three.

Two years later Louis' system of reading and writing was at last accepted. It was to be used throughout France. Slowly the use of *braille*, as it came to be known, spread to other countries.

Further facts

Louis Braille continued to work at his *braille* method, and made it possible to write and read music with *braille*. He also worked out short ways of writing common words.

Thousands of *braille* books are now published each year in many different languages. This computer has a *braille* keyboard and a *braille* display. It can be used by a blind person to write, change and store information. It can print out in *braille* or ordinary print.

The *Braille* Alphabet

A B C D E

F G H I J

K L M N O

P Q R S T

U V W X Y

Z   and   for   of   the

Important dates in Louis' lifetime

1809   Louis Braille is born in France.

1812   Louis has an accident that leaves him blind in one eye.

1813-14 Louis gradually becomes blind in the other eye.

1814   Captain Barbier starts work on his 'Night-writing'.

1816   Louis starts at the village school.

1819   Louis goes to Paris to the Institute for the Blind.

1821   Barbier shows his 'Night-writing' to pupils at the Institute.

1824   Louis completes work on his own first 'dot' alphabet.

1828   Louis is appointed as a teacher at the Institute.

1843   Louis falls ill

1852   Louis dies, aged forty-three.

1854   *Braille* is adopted as the official system for the blind in France.

1878   *Braille* is chosen as the best system for the blind world-wide.